T0170922

DEAR ELIZABETH

On the grounds of Yaddo, May and Elizabeth each have an arm around the painter Beauford Delaney.

DEAR ELIZABETH

Five Poems & Three Letters
to Elizabeth Bishop

MAY SWENSON

Afterword by Kirstin Hotelling Zona

UTAH STATE
UNIVERSITY PRESS
Logan, Utah

Utah State University Press
Logan, UT 84322-7800

Originally Published as *Four Poems and a Letter to Elizabeth Bishop*,
Bear River Press, 1997.

Manufactured in the United States of America.

Library of Congress Cataloging-in-Publication Data

Swenson, May.
  Dear Elizabeth : five poems and three letters to Elizabeth Bishop /
May Swenson ; afterword by Kirstin Hotelling Zona.
    p. cm.
  ISBN: 978-0-87421-296-9
  1. Bishop, Elizabeth, 1911-1979--Poetry. 2. Bishop, Elizabeth,
1911-1979--Correspondence. 3. Poets, American--20th
century--Correspondence. 4. Women poets, American--Correspondence. 5.
Women poets--Poetry. I. Bishop, Elizabeth, 1911-1979. II. Title.
  PS3537.W4786 D43 2000
  811'.54--dc21

                              00-009296

CONTENTS

POEMS

HER EARLY WORK

Talked to cats and dogs,
to trees, and to strangers.
To one loved, talked through
layers of masks.
To this day we can't know
who was addressed,
or ever undressed.
Because of the wraparounds,
overlaps and gauzes,
kept between words and skin,
we notice nakedness.
Wild and heathen scents
of shame or sin
hovered since childhood,
when the delicious was always
forbidden. "A Word With You"
had to be whispered,
spoken at the zoo,
not to be overheard
by eavesdropping ape or cockatoo.

n.d. (begun in 1983)
Published in In Other Words, *1987*

FROM A LETTER
TO ELIZABETH BISHOP

Glancing through your letter again I see your phrase "a child no one knows whether is a boy or a girl," and the note: "You can arrange this to please yourself – it is beyond me right now." So here are my arrangements.

No one knows a child, whether is a boy or a girl.
Or a girl–whether is a boy, a child–no one
    knows.
A child or a girl, no one knows whether is a boy.
A child, whether is a boy, no? One knows, or a
    girl . . .
A child is a boy or a girl? No one knows whether.
Is a boy or a girl a child whether no one knows?
A child? No. One knows whether. Or a girl is a
    boy.

1954

DEAR ELIZABETH

Yes, I'd like a pair of *Bicos de Lacre*—
meaning beaks of "lacquer" or "sealing wax"?
(the words are the same in Portuguese)
". . . about 3 inches long including the tail,
red bills and narrow bright red masks . . ."
You say the male has a sort of "dropping
mandarin-mustache–one black stripe"–

otherwise the sexes are alike. "Tiny but
plump, shading from brown and gray on top
to pale beige, white, and a rose red spot
on the belly"–their feathers, you tell
me, incredibly beautiful "alternating
lights and darks like nearly invisible
wave-marks on a sandflat at low tide,

and with a pattern so fine one must put on
reading glasses to appreciate it properly."
Well, do they sing? If so, I expect their
note is extreme. Not something one hears,
but must watch the cat's ears to detect.
And their nest, that's "smaller than a fist,
with a doorway in the side just wide enough

for each to get into to sleep." They must
be very delicate, not easy to keep. Still,
on the back porch on Perry St., here, I'd
build them a little Brazil. I'd save every
shred and splinter of New York sunshine
and work through the winter to weave them
a bed. A double, exactly their size,

with a roof like the Ark. I'd make sure to
leave an entrance in the side. I'd set it
in among the morning-glories where the
gold-headed flies, small as needles' eyes,
are plentiful. Although "their egg is apt
to be barely as big as a baked bean . . ."
It rarely hatches in captivity, you mean—

but we could hope! In today's letter you
write, "The *Bicos de Lacre* are adorable as
ever—so tiny, neat, and taking baths
constantly in this heat, in about 1/4 inch
of water—then returning to their *filthy*
little nest to lay another egg—which
never hatches." But here it might! And it

doesn't matter that "their voice is weak,
they have no song." I can see them as I
write—on their perch on my porch. "From
the front they look like a pair of half-

ripe strawberries"–except for that stripe.
"At night the cage looks empty" just as
you say. I have "a moment's fright"–

then see the straw nest moving softly.
Yes, dear Elizabeth, if you would be so
kind, I'd like a pair of *Bicos de Lacre*–
especially as in your P.S. you confess,
"I already have two unwed female wild
canaries, for which I must find husbands
in order to have a little song around here."

1965

SOMEBODY WHO'S SOMEBODY

(Draft, never finished; title supplied.)

Somebody who's somebody
    often doesn't look like somebody
until you look
    inside.
Elizabeth's liver is tattooed
    with the intaglio of an indigo turtle.
Not emblazoned–
    that would augur prominence
and a definite who's who-ness
    No–nobodyness is the ultimate
achievement achieved
    secretly, invisibly but indelibly
inside.

(O but remember, E
    I saw you pee on the floor
at Yaddo long ago)
    Enviable that ennoblement
that accrues from the peasant's
    modest and unmodish stance,
the man with the hoe (that's really
    a scepter *inside*),

the low brow that hides
    a hemisphere heapish as a hive.
O golden bees of your eccentric
    thinkishness, each a queen hermited
within–the hairdo like mud
    round the armature of cobwebs,
but mansioned behind that seedy
    facade what a Midas realm,
what orderly glitter, your honey
    mausoleum private
and impenetrable, perfectly
    coned and sealed except for the little
arched bunghole where over the draw
    bridge of your tongue the worker words
pass forth.

But E, remember
    we tried to find Lake Lonely long ago
wandering awkwardly beside
    the yellow reeds, the ditch-black
waters, and played at darts
    in the Paddock Bar by the racetrack.
You read my "Lion" and
    I your "Little Exercise."
You got drunk and snickered, air
    whistled though your teeth at
dinner, everyone thought you were

silly. I burned from head to foot
for you hoping they hadn't
   noticed. Later you peed on
the floor–just a drop or two–at
   West House–because the
bathroom was locked. I felt
   responsible–I should have had
a toilet in my pocket, to produce
   in the moment of your
unpostponable need. I was nuts
   about you. And I couldn't say
a word. And you never said *the*
   word that would have loosened
all my doggy love and let me
   jump you like a suddenly
unhobbled hound wild for love.

Little Elizabeth
   who still keeps me
wild at the end of your chain–because
   I can't reach you, have never
pawed you, slaver at the thought
   of you still, because because
I have never *known* you years
   and years–and love
the unknown you.

1961 or 1962

IN THE BODIES OF WORDS

For Elizabeth Bishop (1911-1979)

Tips of the reeds silver in sunlight. A cold wind
sways them, it hisses through quills of the pines.
Sky is clearest blue because so cold. Birds drop down
in the dappled yard: white breast of nuthatch, slate
catbird, cardinal the color of blood.

Until today in Delaware, Elizabeth, I didn't know
you died in Boston a week ago. How can it be
you went from the world without my knowing?
Your body turned to ash before I knew. Why was there
no tremor of the ground or air? No lightning flick
between our nerves? How can I believe? How grieve?

I walk the shore. Scraped hard as a floor by wind.
Screams of terns. Smash of heavy waves. Wind rips
the corners of my eyes. Salty streams freeze on my face.
A life is little as a dropped feather. Or split shell
tossed ashore, lost under sand. . . . But vision lives!
Vision, potent, regenerative, lives in bodies of words.
Your vision lives, Elizabeth, your words
from lip to lip perpetuated.

Two days have passed. Enough time, I think, for death
to be over. As if your death were not *before* my knowing.

For a moment I jump back to when all was well and ordinary.
Today I could phone to Boston, say hello. . . . Oh, no!
Times's tape runs forward only. There is no replay.

Light hurts. Yet the sky is dull today. I walk the shore.
I meet a red retriever, young, eager, galloping
out on the surf. At first I do not notice his impairment.
His right hind leg is missing. Omens. . . .
I thought I saw a rabbit in the yard this morning.
It was a squirrel, its tail torn off. Distortions. . . .

Ocean is gray again today, old and creased aluminum
without sheen. Nothing to see on that expanse.
Except, far out, low over sluggish waves, a long
clotted black string of cormorants trails south.
Fog-gray rags of foam swell in scallops up the beach,
their outlines traced by a troupe of pipers–
your pipers, Elizabeth!–their racing legs like spokes
of tiny wire wheels.

Faintly the flying string can still be seen.
It swerves, lowers, touching the farthest tips of waves.
Now it veers, appears to shorten, points straight out.
It slips behind the horizon. Vanished.

But vision lives, Elizabeth. Your visions multiplies,
is magnified in the bodies of words.

Not vanished, your vision lives from eye to eye,
your words from lip to lip perpetuated.

Bethany, Delaware
1979

Dear Elizabeth:

I should have written long before this to assure you that you spelled "euphemism" right–I checked it right away, in your former letter–but I have always had this trouble about answering letters–I *never* do it upon getting a letter (which is just when I should do it, because it's at that time only that a spontaneous reply would come out; later on it's a heavier, thought-out reply; it's a symptom of something hesitant and un-free in my make-up–inertia, a gap between thinking and acting always.)

Well, advance copies of my book are printed now and I was up at Rinehart the other day to autograph the complimentary copies (and told them to send yours air mail–so I hope they did.) I think the jacket* is in very bad taste and the picture turned out awful (the larger photo they showed me looked very much better–you could see white in the eyes and the shadows were not as pronounced–it had *some* expression besides the squint, and wasn't so dark altogether. Then they cropped it, too, and the result is it really looks like something in a *cage*.) The print is cramped and hard to read–and it's shockingly over-priced. Well, all that doesn't matter, I guess–it wouldn't if its contents was first-rate. I have no honest idea how I feel about *that* at this point–only conflicting and shifting reactions about it. I do feel, though (and hope it turns true), that when I get to writing again it will be along a very different path–away from *effects.* I think that your comments really pointed to that weakness, in general, and it's something that I've been doing either unconsciously, or over-consciously, that has to be gotten rid of by a changed attitude–by a different posture of mind and feelings. Well, we'll see.

I expect my trip west in a few weeks' time will be good for me, if I can survive those readings. (My hometown U. asked me to read, too) I have four to do, now, and hope there won't be more. We'll be going by bus, and we'll make some side trips into the southwest. I'm looking forward to the visit to my sister and husband and baby in L.A. They have a house that, she says, has every gadget and labor-saving thing ever invented; her husband is a partner in Pacific Jazz Co. which puts out "intellectual" records, too. He recently sent me a record of Gerald Heard lecturing–it's pretty good, too–philosophy for the atom age. Have you ever heard of Heard? I hadn't, and probably should have. (British.)

Our cat is very tall and long now–and vocal. The guppies and other fish had to be disposed of long ago. We are subletting our part of the apartment to two painter friends for two months, and I'm waiting to hear from them (they're in Mexico) as to whether we can leave Z-B with them–if not, it is going to be a problem since the friends in the country who were going to take him have just sold their place. I have to have him altered too, I guess, although he has shown absolutely no signs as yet (10 months old). We'll write you, from the West, Elizabeth and Lotaat least cards. Leaving Sept. 15.

Love to you.

May (& Pearl†)

* The yellow in it is exactly that shade of paint they put in a strip along the gutters here (and subway platforms) to warn you not to miss your step.

---

† *Pearl Schwartz, May's friend and partner at the time.*

Dear Elizabeth (and Lota‡):

Did you know that the world is going to end next week? I trust this will reach you before then. We just heard over the radio that there are rumors originating in Miami–loads of people, mainly teenagers, phoned the police stations there with the warning–it's like the flying saucer reports. Seems to have started as result of a report that a canonized saint, a nun, who received a vision containing predictions on the future of the world in 1919 and was ordered to keep them secret until 1960, was now ready to reveal the predictions.

At New Directions, I happened onto a file of past issues of *The Quarterly Review of Literature* and saw your name on a cover and it was a whole issue devoted to Marianne Moore and I enjoyed your article in it tremendously–I think you have a special flair for writing "criticism"–it is always done in such a penetrating and warm and original way when you do it–witness the Lowell jacket comment, too. Then, of course, I found your new "Brazil" poem in *The New Yorker*. Deceptively plain and just conversational at first–so relaxed in its form–and then with other readings, and read aloud, becoming brilliantly colored and symbolized like the birds and the lizards behind the screening leaves and against the rocks. Like a tapestry, it is not exhibitionistic–a painting often is–it is discrete and there is something utilitarian about it, not just decorative or "expressionistic"–one becomes not so much excited as absorbed. And everything is placed and described accurately, rather than flamboyantly (which

---

‡ *Lota de Macedo Soares, with whom Bishop was living in Brazil.*

would have been easier)–and there is much to see and to find, having to do with time, season, place, history, but all sewed with a very personal yet modest stitch.

Thought you might like to read this "beat" article from *Evergreen Review*–because it's about Billie Holiday.

About the binoculars, I don't really know exactly what the numbers on the right eyepiece mean–except that they are useful as numbers markers. When you've got it adjusted to conform with the left, so that you get a clear image with both eyes, you can keep it set that way and you don't have to change it–just use the center focus for adjusting for distance. The numbers in the center over the "nose bridge" similarly, I guess, are for lining up with the little white dot to find which spread is best for your eyes, and after removing from the case you can always line it up the same way and not have to search for the right eye-spread position. "7" means the depth of vision and that the object is magnified 7 times, while "50" refers to the range or width of vision; a "6 x 30" for instance gives you that much less magnification and width. I wonder if anyone has ever done a *Field Guide to South American Birds.* If I can find one I'll send it to you. We have Peterson's guide to both eastern and western birds–with colored pictures of them all and their field marks–points of identification. Just like the stars are different where you are, the birds are. What an adventurous place to live in!

I can't remember whether I've sent you any of these poems before–I don't think so. "Snow in New York" is going to be in *Poetry* and "From the Office Window" was in *Sat. Review.* "The Pigeon Woman" is a newer one. The ones I did at Yaddo are real *strangies*– I don't know what to make of them yet–different from any of the kinds I've done so far. I find I've accumulated a whole new batch– more than 40–since Fall of '58 when my book came out. I'm putting them together, have been doing all the typing on the finished ones–although I know neither Rinehart or anyone else will want another book from me so soon. But on principle I'm going to apply for an extension of the Guggenheim, and this way I will have something to show them. (I doubt they'll give it to me–but may as well try.) Rinehart has merged with Holt & Co.–did I tell you?–whether this will mean more, or less, interest in poetry publishing I don't know–probably will make no difference. There's a Mary Roberts Rinehart Foundation now, which is new, and they are going to give cash grants to poets for completion of their works–so my editor said I should try for one. Another reason for putting a manuscript together. . . .

I got a pretty good review in the winter issue of *Prairie Schooner.* On the cover it says, "May Swenson's Poetry" (what a guilty jerk of the heart I got seeing that)–by someone I've never heard of, Betty Miller Davis of Fayetteville, Arkansas. It's called "A Certain Coloring" and she considers my book seriously and sort of thoroughly. She didn't "get" everything, but quite a lot. (Must remember to write and thank her.)

French is coming along–I go once a week now, and Pearl is going once a week to Italian. But I listened to a play in French on the radio yesterday–came into the middle of it–and wished there was a knob (like on the dictaphone) that would turn them to slow.

How was your trip and stay in the fishing village? *Who* is doing the watercolors? Is the New York visit definitely off?

> Love to you both,
> May
> and love from Pearl

November 14, 1962

Dear Liz: (Just to make you mad)

I'M not mad at you
So DON'T be mad at me. . .

goes a song by that terrible Frawncis Fay on a campy record that you may have heard. . . ? By a skin's breadth and the hair of your teeth (or a hare's breath and the tin of your skeeth) you got under the wire and will have the distinkshun of decorating the back f-lap of my jack-ette. (I will stop being Jezra Oyce and Pames Jound right now, and talk straight.) Your Registered letter form Petropolis came yesterday just in the tick of nine (sorry)–and your other one postmarked Rio I picked out of the mailbox before stepping into a taxi this morning to go up to Scribner's where, on this very last day, editor was writing jacket copy and had culled juicy old snippets from reviews to fill up the *blank space,* and grabbed your precious words and photostated them and then couldn't read them (but I could and I said why not print the photo with your handwriting exactly as is which I think is a real ridgional idea but he said Niet– too expensive.) The part about the regurgitating owl came out on the second photo and would be propriate, too–there's an owl in the design for the cover. (Don't be afraid, I'm just drunk.) Without having drank anything, thanks. I think I'm just happy. Or thank I'm just hippy! *Stop!*

I like everything you said–the *sub-mundane*–the *ungrudging*–the *nature* and the *sincere* the *buy* and the *read*–editor thinks it is great, too. You are very very kind and I hope I deserve it. I called Lowell's number but no answer, but will phone again before mailing this, so maybe give you some news. You are a darling to send a record of Brazilian birds along with E. H. I'll get holt of it soon as I can. You're a darling period, and a dear exclamation point. And I will write *clearly* soon as I can.

I did phone and talk to Elizabeth Hardwick and will pick up record on my way to doctor on Friday. She said Lowell "is at home now and is completely well"—to reassure you, on that point. Said you must have heard from him since he got home—he's written you. Again 1000 thanks (I'm a little more sober now). Sorry to have caused you such a tizzy—those terrible mails!

Love,
May

AFTERWORD

Urged by the "Unknown You"
May Swenson and Elizabeth Bishop

KIRSTIN HOTELLING ZONA

Between their first meeting in 1950 and Bishop's death in 1979, Bishop and Swenson exchanged over 260 letters. From the start, Swenson's admiration of Bishop was both furrowed and fueled by what she once called Bishop's "cagey" poetics: "'The Shampoo' I like *very* much . . . but I would have a deuce of a time saying why . . . that is, it feels like something has been left out–but this makes it better, in a way . . . a mysteriousness, although the expression is perfectly straightforward" (Sept. 14, 1953). Two years later, Swenson's attempts at provocation have become more explicit:

> I don't understand the Four Poems, that is, I get their
> *mood*, but I can only imagine what they're talking about–my
> imagination goes pretty wild and comes back with strange
> answers . . . Reading these four poems I have to furnish
> them with "meanings" from my own experience because
> you've left yours out. . . . I'm left outside here, sniffing and
> listening, and no use pounding on the door. (August 24,
> 1955)

In replies to these letters, Bishop assured Swenson that her "strange answers" were right on the mark, though their correspondence continued to keep those answers implicit. It is tempting to catalogue the palpable caginess of this correspondence as sexual masking; Swenson and Bishop were both lesbians who would not lodge themselves within a growing field of woman-identified poetry, and maintaining this distance, perhaps, made them wary of identifying with each other in these terms. Moreover, as the unfinished love-poem included here suggests, their friendship had the potential, at least from Swenson's perspective, for sexual intimacy. To acknowledge openly the relationship between one's "cagey" poems and one's desire may well have meant sacrificing the distance that, ironically, allowed them to maintain their friendship over the years.

> . . . I was nuts
> about you. And I couldn't say
> a word. And you never said *the*
> word that would have loosened
> all my doggy love . . .

wrote Swenson in the poem she never showed to Bishop. Whether or not Swenson's feelings were reciprocated (and I have found nothing in Bishop's archive that suggests they were), Bishop was clearly unwilling to unleash the "hound wild for love" that she most likely detected in her friend. At the same time, though, Swenson's attraction to Bishop turned upon this very resistance; although she seemed to long at times for a more forthright and open communion with Bishop, Swenson was drawn insatiably to the process of *implication* in which their relationship was rooted:

        Little Elizabeth
who still keeps me
        wild at the end of your chain–
        . . . because because
I have never *known* you years
        and years–and love
the unknown you.

Read in isolation, this confession seems to be a response to
unrequited love, a hunger for the hard-to-get. But if we consider it
alongside the published poems that Swenson wrote about Bishop
and the letters from which these poems were gleaned, this admission
reveals a mind far more complex. Though Swenson was frustrated at
times by as Bishop's "prudish ears" (Oct. 21, 1970), she was
inspired deeply by her friend's ability to produce poems with a
"casual and absolutely natural tone," poems that are "very honest,"
that "never call attention to their effects" (August 24, 1955).
Swenson struggled to name this combination of down-to-earth
sincerity and "cagey" self-restraint in a letter she wrote to Bishop in
1955:

    your poems . . . engage something else than the
    emotions. What is it? Something else, and something more
    important. They are hard, feelable, as objects–or they give
    us that sensation–and they are separate from the self that
    made them, rather than self-effigies as poems easily tend to
    be. (August 24, 1955)

Over the years, Swenson softened her attempts to extract
"meanings" from Bishop; her letters become less urgent, her

frustrations more covert. At the same time, however, Swenson refined her *own* caginess–both in her letters to Bishop and her poems at large–in an effort to achieve the "something else . . ." that so inspired her.

For this reason, I find Swenson's middle and later letters to Bishop (three of which are included in this booklet) in many ways the most interesting. Here we find Swenson at her riddling best:

> I should have written long before this to assure you that
> you spelled 'euphemism' right–I checked it right away, in
> your former letter–but I have always had this trouble about
> answering letters–I *never* do it upon getting a letter (which
> is just when I *should* do it, because it's at that time only that
> a spontaneous reply would come out . . .) (August 14,
> 1958)

An earlier ("spontaneous"?) Swenson would have insisted more overtly on the irony of Bishop's self-consciousness in this context. Instead, Swenson does so "euphemistically," and I think more effectively. By assuring Bishop that she has spelled "euphemism" correctly–and moreover, that she "looked it up right away" (something, of course, that Bishop could have done herself)–Swenson artfully mirrors the characteristic of Bishop that both fascinates and frustrates her most,

> . . . that ennoblement
> that accrues from the peasant's
> modest and unmodish stance,
> the man with the hoe (that's really
> a scepter *inside*)

In other words, Swenson is coming to terms with the *power* of restraint, and in doing so, she learns to refine her poetry "away from *effects*" (August 14, 1958).

This progression in Swenson's work is condensed and intensified in the poems she wrote about Bishop. There is something strangely unnerving, even self-serving, about Bishop's reticence that Swenson's writing asks us to see, and perhaps no poem says this more overtly than the unfinished one published here. Clearly this poem is a rough one; it is syntactically messy and emotionally disjointed. But these characteristics are symptomatic of the difficult feelings Swenson was attempting to process in the poem, feelings that have less to do with *Bishop's* reticence than with Swenson's life-long fascination with *reticence* itself. I like this poem for its rawness, its incompleteness–for those qualities that render it unpublishable in ordinary contexts. Alongside the other poems in this collection, "Somebody" becomes a source of backlighting; it illuminates the published poems by accentuating their shadows, the unspoken tensions upon which they turn.

Like all of Swenson's best pieces, these poems explore the *contexts* out of which our conclusions emerge–the heterosexual trimmings that line the ark-like nest of the *Bicos de Lacre,* the "distortions" that echo the disturbing distance of "In the Bodies of Words," the "layers of masks" through which "A Word With You" was whispered at the zoo. It is common practice today to emphasize Bishop's honesty at the expense of her restraint, as if the one contradicted the other, but Swenson's incisive imagination asks us to recognize the ways in which they go hand in hand. A life-long lover of riddles, Swenson understood that explicitness often works against the process of revelation that poetry should engender:

[T]he poetic experience is one of constant curiosity,
skepticism, and testingastonishment, disillusionment,
renewed discovery, re-illumination. It amounts to a virtual
compulsion to probe with the senses into the complex
actuality of all things, outside and inside the self and to
determine relationships between them.[*]

To emphasize the self that is seeing instead of the thing being seen is, Swenson knew, to curtail the discoveries that a poem might otherwise spark. We encounter the wisdom of this perspective in "Her Early Work":

Because of the wraparounds,
overlaps and gauzes,
kept between words and skin,
we notice nakedness.

"Masks," "overlaps," and "gauzes" do not only hide–they have the power to reveal, to emphasize, to help us "notice nakedness." This understanding grants Bishop's "whispered" words a conscious agency, and hence respect, that they are sometimes denied; while Bishop clearly struggled against the confines of heterosexist culture, her poetics of restraint can't be chocked up to coded cries of repression. On the contrary, her silences were often strategic, in the service of unearthing assumptions instead of giving answers. To think of poetry as a form of power is to recognize the productive aspect of "cagey" descriptions, to understand that observations are never innocent.

---

[*] *May Swenson, "The Experience of Poetry in a Scientific Age," Poets on Poetry, ed. Howard Nemerov (New York: Basic Books, 1966) 148.*

Herein thrives the enormous heart of Swenson's poetry: she reveled in the *energies* of language, its organic pulse and its capacity for change. To Swenson, language was alive, breathing, expanding, contracting. It had texture, taste, a sensuality that risks the rawest pain just as it summons ecstasy. In this way, poetry, like the process of living from which it is inextricable, is a continual source of *hope*, which is why Swenson's poems are ripe with laughter. It is for this reason that I chose to conclude this collection with the uncharacteristically irreverent letter of November 14, 1962. Of all the correspondence Swenson shared with Bishop, this piece is the giddiest, the most playful, reminding me of what it is about Swenson that makes her work so enduring. In this letter, she is thanking Bishop for her dust-jacket comments on *To Mix With Time* (1963), and the pleasure she derived from Bishop's compliments is typically contagious. But in pairing the poems with this letter I mean to stress something more as well–that Swenson's electrifying optimism cannot be disentangled from her shrewd, unsparing eye, her distinctive ability to bring life to the most subtle and "cagey" of signs. And at the heart of this junction, as at the core of the friendship these pages commend, prevails the poetry itself: *"Vision, potent, regenerative, lives in bodies of words."*

Somebody who's somebody
often doesn't look like somebody
until you look
    inside
Elizabeth's liver is tatooed
with the intaglio of an indigo turtle
    Not emblazoned
That would augur prominence
and a definite who's whoness
No — nobodyness is the ultimate
achievement achieved
secretly, invisibly but indelibly
    inside

(O but remember, E
    I saw you pee
    on the floor at yaddo long ago)
Enviable that enrollment
that accrues from the peasants'
modest & immodish stance the
    man with the hoe (that's really
a scepter inside)